Fish

CHELSEA CLUBHOUSE

An Imprint of Chelsea House Publishers
A Haights Cross Communications Company

Philadelphia

June Loves

This edition first published in 2004 in the United States of America by Chelsea Clubhouse, a division of Chelsea House Publishers and a subsidiary of Haights Cross Communications.

Chelsea Clubhouse
1974 Sproul Road, Suite 400
Broomall, PA 19008-0914

The Chelsea House world wide web address is www.chelseahouse.com

First published in 2003 by
MACMILLAN EDUCATION AUSTRALIA PTY LTD
627 Chapel Street, South Yarra, Australia, 3141

Associated companies and representatives throughout the world.

Copyright © June Loves 2003
Copyright in photographs © individual photographers as credited

Page layout by Domenic Lauricella
Photo research by Legend Images

Printed in China

Acknowledgements
The author and the publisher are grateful to the following for permission to reproduce copyright material:

Cover photograph: boy with pet goldfish in bowl, courtesy of ANT Photo Library.

ANT Photo Library, pp. 1, 4, 8–9; Jean-Michel Labat/Auscape, p. 7; Labat-Lanceau/Auscape, pp. 5, 15; Yvette Tavernier—Bios/Auscape, pp. 6, 11; Nigel Clements, pp. 27, 28, 29; Coo-ee Picture Library, p. 10; Getty Images, p. 30; Legend Images, pp. 23, 25; MEA Photo, p. 17 (scissors, scraper, sieve); Photography Ebiz, pp. 14, 21, 22, 24, 26; Photomax, p. 12 (bottom); Dale Mann/Retrospect, pp. 16–17, 18, 19, 20; Dave Thompson, pp. 12 (top), 13.

With special thanks to The Pines Pet Centre, The Ark.

While every care has been taken to trace and acknowledge copyright, the publisher tenders their apologies for any accidental infringement where copyright has proved untraceable. Where the attempt has been unsuccessful, the publisher welcomes information that would redress the situation.

Contents

Fish

Fish are quiet pets. They are excellent pets for people who live in apartments or small houses.

Goldfish are a common pet fish.

Goldfish are pet fish that live in cool water. Guppies are **tropical** pet fish that live in warm water.

Many tropical fish can live together in a warm-water tank.

Kinds of Fish

There are many kinds, sizes, shapes, and colors of pet fish. Their heads, eyes, tails, and fins may look different depending on the type of fish.

Many pet fish are brightly colored.

Goldfish

Some goldfish are orange. Others are a mixture of orange, black, and white.

Kinds of goldfish

- ✪ common
- ✪ comet
- ✪ fantail
- ✪ veiltail
- ✪ black moor

Some owners keep a variety of goldfish.

Parts of a Fish

A fish is a **vertebrate** that lives in water. Most fish have the same body parts as goldfish.

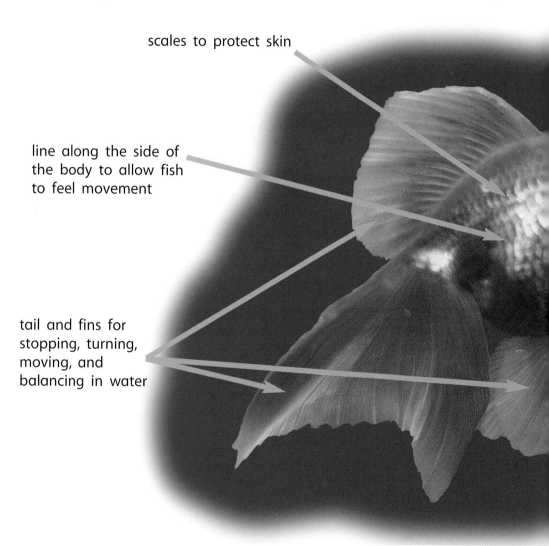

scales to protect skin

line along the side of the body to allow fish to feel movement

tail and fins for stopping, turning, moving, and balancing in water

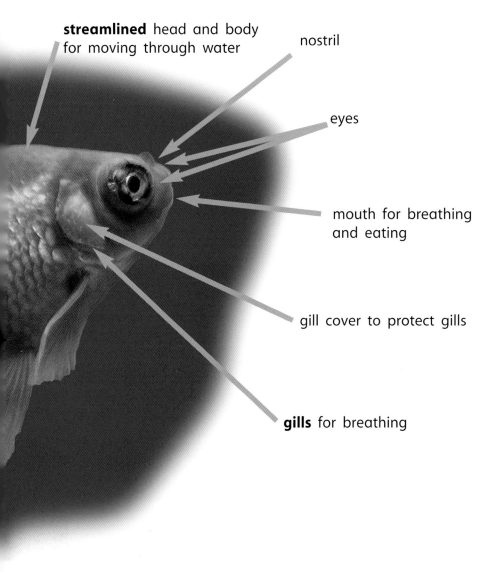

streamlined head and body
for moving through water

nostril

eyes

mouth for breathing
and eating

gill cover to protect gills

gills for breathing

Breathing

Fish take in **oxygen** from the water.
Water goes in through the fish's mouth.
As the water passes over the gills,
oxygen is taken into the blood.

A fish takes in water through its mouth to get oxygen.

Fish move their bodies and tails to swim.

Moving

Fish push themselves through the water with their bodies and tails. They curve their streamlined bodies and swish their tails. Fish use their fins to steer, stop, and balance in the water.

Young Fish

Baby fish are called fry. Some fish lay eggs that hatch in the water. Other fish give birth to live fry that can already swim. The eggs hatch inside the mother fish.

The female goldfish lays thousands of tiny eggs. If **fertilized**, the eggs hatch after three or four days.

The tiny fry has an egg sack attached to its body. After two or three days the fry has used up the egg sack as food.

After four months,
the fry is about 1 inch
(2.5 centimeters) long.

After about six months,
the young goldfish's
body changes color.

Choosing Pet Fish

Choose fish that are active and healthy. The number and kind of fish you choose will depend on the size and shape of your tank.

Make sure all fish in the tank look healthy before picking one.

If you have a big tank, add only one or two fish every two weeks. This gives the **bacteria** that destroy harmful **waste** time to grow in your tank.

Fish need plenty of space to move around in.

Caring for Pet Fish

Set up a tank before you bring your pet fish home. These are some of the supplies you may want to care for your pet fish.

a wide tank or bowl

water plants to keep the water healthy

an electric **air pump** and **water filter** to keep the tank water clean and fresh

wood or ornaments

gravel or sand for the bottom of the tank

scissors to trim plants

Rocks, wood, and ornaments make good hiding and resting places for fish.

rocks and stones of different sizes, colors, and shapes

sieve to wash gravel

siphon to vacuum gravel and remove dirty water and waste

soft net to catch fish

scrubbing brush to scrub the tank and equipment

scraper to clean glass

Setting up the tank

Place the tank on a strong stand or table away from heaters and bright sunlight.

Make sure your tank is clean.

What to do

- ✪ Clean the tank, rocks, wood, and other ornaments.
- ✪ Clean and rinse the gravel, then gently pour it into the tank.
- ✪ If you have a water filter or air pump, set it up according to directions.
- ✪ Wash plants gently and plant in the gravel.
- ✪ Place rocks, wood, and other ornaments on the gravel.
- ✪ Gently fill your tank halfway, then fill to just below the top.
- ✪ Let the tank stand for a week before buying your fish.

Live water plants will help to keep the water clean.

Keeping Tropical Fish

Tropical fish need to live in a warm-water tank. The water temperature should be the same as in their natural **habitat**.

You may need to test the tank's water to make sure it is safe for your fish.

What you need

- a tank
- a tank heater
- tropical water plants
- gravel
- an air pump and a water filter
- rocks and other ornaments
- a siphon for cleaning.

Keeping Outdoor Fish

Cold-water fish, such as goldfish, can live in a pond in the garden. Fish can live for a long time in a pond if you feed them the right food and the water is healthy.

Some pond fish can grow quite large.

What you need

A mesh covering over the pond will protect fish from birds and other pets.

plants around the edge of the pond   pond liner   water plants

Bringing Pet Fish Home

Bring your pet fish home in a plastic bag. Float the bag in the tank. Leave it for at least 20 minutes until the water temperature in the bag is the same as the water temperature in the tank. Gently let your fish swim free.

Use a plastic bag to take your fish home.

Feeding

Feed pet fish a pinch of dried flake food or pellets every day. Fish will also nibble on plants and **algae**. You can buy fish food from a pet store or supermarket.

There are many kinds of fish food.

25

Treats

Some types of pet fish may eat small insects or pond animals. If you skim a net through a pond, you can collect water beetles and other pond life for your fish to eat. Put the insects and small animals in the tank for your fish.

Ponds are a good place to find live food for some types of pet fish.

Cleaning the Tank

Take out uneaten food, dead plant leaves, and fish droppings from the water. Remove any algae from the glass with a scraper. Top up the tank with fresh water every few weeks.

Add water to your tank when needed.

Training

You can train your pet fish to know when it is dinner time. Sprinkle food carefully in one side of the bowl. Gently tap the side or ring a bell to signal that it is dinner time.

Try to feed your fish at the same time every day.

Visiting the Vet

If your fish look sick, take them to your **vet** for advice and care. To keep your pet fish healthy you must give them the right food and keep the tank and water clean.

A strong plastic bag is a safe way to take your fish to the vet.

In the Wild

In the wild, fish live in oceans, rivers, streams, and lakes. Marine fish live in sea water. Other fish live in fresh water. Many fish swim together in groups called schools.

Large groups of fish are called schools.

Glossary

air pump	an electric pump that puts air into the water
algae	tiny green plants that live in water
bacteria	small living things; some types of bacteria help to keep a fish tank clean
fertilized	able to produce young; a male goldfish spreads a liquid over the female's eggs to fertilize them
gills	parts of a fish's body that take in oxygen from water
habitat	the place where animals or plants live
oxygen	a colorless gas in air or water, which animals need to breathe
sieve	a fine mesh that liquid can be poured through
siphon	a tube used to drain water out of a tank
streamlined	shaped to move easily through the water
tropical	coming from or living in a place with hot temperatures
vertebrate	an animal with a backbone
vet	a doctor who treats animals; short for veterinarian
waste	harmful material such as uneaten food, dead plant leaves, and fish droppings
water filter	a device that keeps water clean and clear

Index